Top Tips for

# MANAGERS OF

# WORKING PARENTS

**Top Tips for**

# MANAGERS OF

# WORKING PARENTS

**Jo Lyon and Chris Parke**

Matador
9 Priory Business Park,
Wistow Road, Kibworth Beauchamp,
Leicestershire. LE8 0RX
Tel: (+44) 116 279 2299
Fax: (+44) 116 279 2277
Email: books@troubador.co.uk
Web: www.troubador.co.uk/matador

ISBN 978-1780883-465

British Library Cataloguing in Publication Data.
A catalogue record for this book is available from the British Library.

Typeset in 12pt Verdana by Troubador Publishing Ltd, Leicester, UK
Printed and bound in the UK by TJ International, Padstow, Cornwall

**Matador** is an imprint of Troubador Publishing Ltd

# About the Authors

Jo Lyon and Chris Parke are co-founders of Talking Talent, an innovative coaching organisation specialising in helping women throughout their careers, as well as supporting men through the transition into fatherhood.

Jo Lyon has over a decade of coaching experience and is both an Occupational Psychologist and a qualified Neuro Linguistic Programming (NLP) coach. She has worked for a wide range of FTSE 100 companies in a variety of sectors, and has coached extensively at all levels. She enjoys helping individuals to maximize their potential and to achieve personal and organisational goals.

Chris Parke started his career in investment banking with BZW, and then moved into consulting with PwC. His interest in leadership psychology and helping teams and individuals realise their full potential drew him towards executive coaching, which he has been delivering for over a decade, specialising in coaching senior individuals and HIPO's. He has a Diploma in Clinical Organisational Psychology from INSEAD and an MBA from Imperial College London.

Chris has written and featured in articles about coaching senior women for the FT, Lawyer Magazine, Women in Banking and Finance, The Director, and HRD. He has also participated as an expert panellist for BBC Television and Radio.

# About Talking Talent

Talking Talent is a niche coaching consultancy which helps companies to:

- Retain and progress their talented women through the "pinch points" in their careers

- Support and develop employees who are working parents as well as their managers.

**Why?**

- Take a look at the first chapter of this book to know more.

**How?**

We use three approaches:

- One-to-one and group coaching: giving individuals a safe space to figure out how to navigate change.

- Development programs: rich, highly interactive workshops which enhance behaviours and increase skills.

- Leading edge technology solutions to support our coaching interventions.

## Want to find out more?

Contact us at www.talking-talent.com or on 01865 400087

# Acknowledgements

The authors would like to acknowledge everyone who helped in putting together this Top Tips book, including all the Talking Talent team. A particular thanks to Tamsin Slyce for her contributions to many of the chapters and to Harriet Beveridge for her help in editing the content. Thanks to Astrid van Waveren for bringing it all together, Vanessa Corley for co-ordinating key parts – and our partners at OneFish TwoFish for the images we have included. Finally we would also like to extend our thanks to all the women and men who have participated in our managers' coaching programmes, shown commitment to supporting their colleagues and teams, and who have given such encouraging feedback.

# Contents

# Introduction

Managing a complex transition, such as maternity, paternity or adoption, can be a daunting task for managers. At times it may seem full of potential pitfalls, but taking the time and effort to manage the transition well can make all the difference in the engagement and effectiveness of the individual and the broader team.

Each transition will be unique, so look at the tips in this book and see which ones are right for you, and the individual you are managing. Leave those which don't feel appropriate for your situation.

The purpose of this book is to help you explore best practice and think about how to make this transition a smooth one.

When working through each section, start to think about:

• What are the most important things for you, the individual and the team?
• What do you need to stop doing?
• What do you need to start doing?
• What do you need to do more of?

**This book is...**

• A treasure trove of hints and tips to help you manage the transition.

- Insights from specialist coaches, senior professionals and experienced managers.
- An encapsulation of the key topics we've helped thousands of individuals and their managers to address in the last seven years.
- A self-coaching resource to help you reflect on and apply the tips to your context.

**How this book is structured...**

The book is arranged around 5 sections.

For each section there is:

- Guidance on relevant topics.
- Practical tips.
- Some coaching questions. These are questions you can ask yourself, to help you think more deeply on the topic and unlock your own answers.

**There will be some sections in this book that may not apply to you and your organisation, please remember to check with your HR contact about your company's policy and current employment law.**

# SECTION 1:

# Areas of focus which are relevant throughout the transition

# Culture and context

*Summary:*
**The commercial implications of losing talent are vast, and can frequently be avoided through effective line management. Understanding the individual, team and organisational context of the leave you will be managing will help you to provide better support to your colleague and team.**

Talking Talent has engaged with many organisations and managers since 2005 and has found that attrition of both male and female staff has been connected to starting a family. Some of those who are planning on starting a family can't see how having children and working will be compatible for them in their current working environment.

## Why it's important to retain working parents:

- **Loss of talented, experienced people**: the number of parents leaving throughout the transition and 1 to 3 years after their return to work can rise to as high as 50%, representing a significant drain on talent.

- **Cost to the business**: the loss of talent means a considerable cost to the business. Recruitment costs, training costs, business disruption, lost knowledge, lost clients, a reliance on less talented replacements – the direct and indirect costs are significant.

- **Hard to cover and replace talent**: organisations invest huge amounts of time and money in training and developing talent. Often talented employees are in positions which make them valuable to the business, department and team and thus hard to cover and replace.

- **Not just a gender issue**: to date this has mainly affected women. However, with the introduction of extended paternity leave in the UK (in April 2011) this may start to change.

- **The benefits of gender diverse organisations:** including better performance, better team work, improved understanding of all client groups, improved marketing and more engaged employees.

- **Higher employee engagement and loyalty**: when maternity, paternity or adoption leave is managed well it can have a significantly positive impact on employee engagement levels and employee loyalty to the business. The positive effects on productivity and client delivery are well publicised, not only for the individual but also for the team around them.

# The role of the line manager

The line manager is fundamental in ensuring maternity, paternity and adoption transitions are well managed and that the individual has a clear sense of his or her accountabilities.

If we work in an environment where there are a lot of working parents we may have a different perspective than if we work in an environment where no one else has children. Thinking through the roles and expectations in our department and team can help us to understand where there may be a need for extra support. If our team works long hours, this may be difficult in the late stages of pregnancy and when the individual returns. Are there any unwritten rules around what people have to do to be good at what they are doing in your organisation?

How might the economic and market conditions affect people's reaction to someone going on leave? It could provide an opportunity for another team member to take on a new challenge, however it may create a sense of uncertainty for our colleague going on leave.

Building a full picture of the context, the individual and the environment around them will help shape how we manage the transition and the conversations that need to happen. The most powerful thing we can do as a manager of people during these transitions is to listen, understand and communicate.

This guide will explore some best practices for the line manager.

Before you read on it is worth reflecting on your organisation, department and team using the coaching questions below to help clarify the culture and context in which the maternity or paternity transition fits.

## Top tips

1. Recognise the context and be prepared to challenge it – just because it has been done one way before doesn't mean it has to be the same this time.

2. Find and share the positive stories, where the transition has been well managed.

3. Support your colleague in identifying any appropriate role models within your area or the wider organisation.

## Coaching questions

1. How good is your organisation, department or team at retaining talent?

2. How many women and men go on maternity, paternity or adoption leave each year? What reputation does your organisation have surrounding the management of leave and what are some of the stories and myths that people share?

3. How much does/would it cost for you to replace one of your key team members?

4.  What impact would it have on your team if you lost a good performer?

5.  What policies and practices are there to support working parents, for example; extensions of maternity benefits, emergency childcare, childcare vouchers, etc?

6.  Is this your first time managing maternity? Paternity? Adoption?

7.  If it isn't how did the previous experience go? What went well and what could have been better? What would the colleague that you managed say?

8.  Is this the first time your colleague has been through maternity, paternity or adoption? If not, what was his/her previous experience like, even if it wasn't with your organisation?

9.  What has your colleague shared about their family and financial context which might impact their options and choices?

10. Have there been other maternity, paternity or adoption cases in the last 3 years on your team or in the department? Is there any "maternity fatigue"? Have the transitions been a success? What would others say about the management of these transitions? What could have been better?

11. How supportive is the organisation to working parents? How about your team?

12. Are there other working parents on your team? Are there visible role models for working parents?

13. How many people work flexibly in your team and department? How will this inform the expectations of the returning parent?

14. How well resourced is your team right now? How well can it cope with a maternity, paternity or adoption leave?

15. How stable is the current team? Do they know each other well? What are the dynamics?

16. Have there been any reorganisations recently? Did they result in redundancies?

17. Where is your colleague in his/her career lifecycle? Is he/she coming up for a promotion?

*"We support staff through the transition to motherhood and are trying to keep our most valuable assets."*

**Vivienne Hole, HRD**

# 2

# Unconscious biases

**Summary:**
**Unconscious biases are a combination of attitudes, experiences, cultural norms and expectations that everyone holds, and they are unique to each of us. As a manager it is important to understand your view of the world and the unconscious biases you hold. By reflecting on your own attitudes and assumptions about maternity, paternity and adoption, as well those of your employees, you can better understand where each person is coming from and how to best support them. If we judge others by our own views we could be well intentioned but miss the real point.**

Our worldview is shaped by where we come from, our cultural norms, our family members, friends and colleagues and their attitudes and assumptions. We have our own unique set of experiences, assumptions and perspectives, which influence who we are, our values, how we react and how we behave.

If we have previously managed a team member, who has had a difficult or easy time, this might influence our reaction to the next person who announces their pregnancy. The reaction an individual gets when they ask to take additional paternity leave may also be conditioned by the fact that few men have taken extended amounts of time after the birth of their children.

If a manager has themself had an easy pregnancy, they may unthinkingly assume their colleague's experience will be similar and may not understand the challenges if their colleague is very sick during pregnancy. Equally, if someone has previously gone into labour early this could make us more focused on handover and may make the person we are managing feel that we are pushing them out early.

If we have doubts about the effectiveness of flexible working, our instant response to someone's application may be negative, without listening to the individual's business case and recommendations. It is important therefore to ask the questions, listen and not to make assumptions.

As a line manager it is also useful to consider what is driving the employee's hopes and fears surrounding the transition. It is a common mistake to "over associate" with the woman moving through maternity. We may project our own values and experiences onto their present situation through our management style or advice provided. Most of the time this is done from a position of trying to be helpful. We could be thinking, *"this is what worked for me; this is how I have seen others make it work."*

It is useful to offer observations on best practice and what has worked, but equally to spend time listening to the circumstances and preferences of our colleague. This will help us provide support and advice that is relevant to **them**.

## Assumptions to challenge

The hardest parts of managing the dynamics within a

diverse team are some of the unconscious or conscious biases that may exist. What are your organisation's unconscious biases – the unsaid rules, expectations or views?

Below are some of the common assumptions and biases to look out for. They may need exploring, challenging or managing:

- Having working parents on the team means non-parents will have to pick up the inevitable slack.

- Flexible or different working patterns are less productive.

- Women returning after maternity leave are no longer career-focused.

- All maternity returners will want more flexibility and need support around achieving work-life balance.

- Working parents always leave early so others will always have to stay late.

- Part time workers put pressure on other team members.

- Working parents are always taking time out for sick children.

- I had to manage through this as a working parent – why can't you?

Notice your reaction to these; how do they sit with you? If you came across these assumptions, what would you do about them? Think about how you can handle these types of views.

**Top tips**

1.   Be aware of your biases and assumptions. Think through the coaching questions below.

2.   Ask trusted colleagues to explore with you any unconscious biases they notice.

3.   Consider how these perceptions could impact on your approach to managing maternity, paternity and adoption transitions.

4.   Understand the unconscious biases others have. Ask appropriate questions and challenge assumptions.

**Coaching questions**

1.   What cultural background do you come from and what influence does this have on your ideal image of the family model?

2.   What is the culture of your business in its support of working parents?

3.   What are your experiences of working with working parents?

4.   What are your thoughts on working women?

5.   What are your thoughts on men taking paternity leave?

6. What are your reflections on people taking extended time out of the business?

7. What is your family model? Does your partner work?

8. What do you think is a good solution for working families?

9. What messages do you want to give to colleagues?

10. What behaviours do you want to display to the team?

11. What tone do you want to set around maternity, paternity, adoption and working parents?

3

# Communication

*Summary:*
**Proactive communication is the most important factor in managing the maternity, paternity and adoption transition. When issues do occur it is often as a result of poor or misinterpreted communication. To be communicating effectively is to be asking questions, listening, displaying empathy and understanding, and not making assumptions around what people want. It's about communicating regularly and in a timely way, with openness and honesty.**

There is nothing that can affect a transition so much as the effectiveness of how individuals communicate with each other – from the line manager, the HR professional, the employee, to the extended team. Many managers are unsure of what to say or do. The most common mistake made by line managers is under-communicating during the transition, which can either be misconstrued as a lack of interest or as an affirmation that *"my career will no longer be seen as a priority now I have announced my leave"*. Poor communication can lead to assumptions being made and sometimes will result in more minor issues being magnified and becoming major problems. This can ultimately lead to business and team disruption.

Much of this book deals with best practices in communication when an individual is going through a maternity, paternity or adoption transition. The suggestions apply to the extended team, which can so often be overlooked, as well as other key stakeholders such as clients and suppliers. Maternity, paternity or adoption leave are not easy transitions to manage as every individual moving through this experience has a unique set of drivers and circumstances influencing the choices and preferences they have. As such, it is impossible to second-guess exactly what each individual will want, particularly as priorities can so quickly shift at each of the different stages of the transition, as we will see. This is why communication is so important.

This, combined with the speed with which businesses change, demands that the manager communicates often, with agility and with empathy. The manager needs to offer support and to be prepared to make considered challenges where appropriate.

Lack of confidence can be a real problem for managers of employees transitioning into parenthood, particularly if they have never managed this type of transition before, or they are not a working parent themselves. Some of the greatest issues surrounding the management of these leaves come from managers who are terrified of doing or saying the wrong thing for fear of looking ill-informed or, worse, finding themselves on the wrong end of a grievance. Often this leads to them taking a step back and communicating less.

Some hold the belief that it is safer not to communicate than to say something that may be misconstrued. This is often the worst stance that the manager can take. A lack of communication will lead to issues in the handover of work and business continuity and in many cases will only serve to feed the fear that some women, and indeed men, have that they may be sidelined after they have announced their leave.

The confidence of women and men returning from maternity, paternity or adoption leave is often down to the individual and what is going on internally for them, but there is no doubt that key people can also shape their experience.

So what can we do as a manager to help maintain communication and keep a confident working parent in our team?

**Top tips**

1. If anything over-communicate, don't take a step back.

2. Remember that others in the team will be looking to you as an example.

3. Individuals who stay in touch with the business when they are away have a more positive return to the office. Encourage them to put a plan in place; who will they keep in touch with, how, when and how often?

4. Update them about significant changes and developments when they are away.

5. Encourage them to connect with you and other key stakeholders at all stages.

6.  Get them to reach out to other working parents and find role models.

7.  Support them by providing coaching so they can manage their hopes and fears, take control of their transition and maintain career momentum.

8.  Recognise what some of their hopes and fears are around becoming a working parent.

9.  Be clear what your hopes and fears are around your colleague leaving and think of positive ways that these can be reframed so that you can share them and manage them.

10. React to any challenges and concerns they have in a timely way.

11. Define clear objectives at each stage and review progress on these.

12. Set realistic expectations and manage the expectations of others.


**Coaching questions**

1.  What is your approach to communicating with your team members?

2.  To support the individual through this transition, what do you need to build on and what do you need to adjust?

3.  To lead the team through this transition, what do

you need to build on and what do you need to adjust?

4.  How do you want to develop your reputation as a manager in the organisation?

5.  What support do you need to feel confident in your communication?

*"I have managed 3 employees through maternity previously, and communication is key!"*

**Caroline Gulliver, Manager, Ernst & Young**

# SECTION 2:

# Preparing for leave

# 4

# Managing from announcement to leave

*Summary:*
**When managing a maternity, paternity or adoption leave, it is never too soon to start planning, even if it is just working out when to have conversations about key milestones. Throughout the time the individual is preparing for leave you need to be aware of the needs of all the key stakeholders including the individual and the team. Early on, discuss with your colleague how they want to handle both communication with others and handing over their work. Consider also the timing of these.**

## Initial announcement and communication with stakeholders

Individuals may have mixed feelings as they announce their leave, some will be excited, some surprised and some worried. Many may be concerned about telling us – their manager – and unsure about how we are going to react or how to tell us. On a personal level they may be wondering what will happen to their career, or even feel guilty that in some way their news may be letting us and the team down. This is particularly true if they are one of the first in their team or have seen others get a disappointing response in the past. For men who are asking for additional paternity leave there may be no precedent yet established. Individuals will have many concerns: *"Will people be pleased, upset, surprised or disappointed? Will they feel let down? And how will this influence how people think about me?"*

It rarely feels like a good time to take a period of extended leave and we have no control over it. Therefore, the way we are perceived to react to the news is important and will set the tone for the forthcoming months. We can then move on to the practical management of the maternity, paternity or adoption leave to ensure we have business continuity. Be positive and don't ask too many questions straight away, it is unlikely the individual will have all the answers yet; they are probably just getting used to the idea of becoming a parent.

On-going communication with stakeholders is critical to the success of working parents. One of the immediate tasks may be helping our colleague to think through how best to share the news of their leave with other stakeholders. It is inevitable that a period of time out is going to impact on a number of people, particularly if the individual works in a team and has direct reports. For some it will be a positive thing as they will be given extra exposure and responsibility, for others it will mean more work or even a different manager.

It can be useful to draw a stakeholder map of key people who will be impacted and who need to be made aware of the upcoming leave. This will include team members, internal and external clients, project teams, career sponsors and senior managers among others.

Consider what order stakeholders should be informed. It may be prudent, for example, to think closely about how and when to inform clients so that they receive the news in a timely and well thought-out way, with early reflections on who will support them during the leave. We may be able to help identify the key stakeholders who need to be told first.

---

**Understanding stakeholder needs**
It is essential to consider who is key to making the transition a success. Who are the potential enablers, the people critical to success both inside and outside of work? Who might be more challenging and how might they be managed? For those returning from maternity, paternity or adoptive leave with constraints on their time, there can be a tendency to place all energy into delivering and getting the job done. This can come at the expense of stakeholder management and the vital visibility of that work and the successes. This in turn can impact career progress.

---

**Top tips**

1. Talk with the individual about how they are currently managing their stakeholders.

2. Suggest to the employee they draw a map of their stakeholders, such as internal or external

clients, suppliers and key internal sponsors. How might each be impacted? What support may be needed from them?

3. Discuss the most appropriate order to inform people.

4. Encourage your colleague to think clearly and commercially about how to approach conversations. What messages do they want to convey? What actions do they need to take?

5. Identify if there are any challenging stakeholders. Consider how your support could influence a positive outcome.

6. Ask the individual to provide regular feedback on what is and is not working. Do the same yourself.

7. Remember you are a leader and role model. Set a supportive tone and the culture. Reinforce constructive messages and behaviours.

8. Address any concerns you have and discuss solutions. Don't just hope for the best.

## Coaching questions

1. What do you and the individual want the various stakeholders to think, feel and do?

2. How can you work together to achieve these outcomes?

## Emotions

When an individual is planning to go on maternity, paternity or adoption leave, they may experience a wide range of emotions from anxiety to excitement and fear. Some may be excited about becoming a parent, but they could also be concerned about letting down their colleagues or clients down, relinquishing control, handing over work or clients they are passionate about or missing out on interesting projects. They may feel sidelined. All of these factors can start to erode the individual's self-image as a respected professional. To remain professional they may also go into denial and not really focus on the fact that they are going on leave for a period until it is very late. It is vital to ensure the person feels involved in the handover and to start the process early. Above all make sure they are realistic about handing over their role in a timely way. We may need to provide support in the handover plan.

For some leavers, there can be a real worry about letting go of work or clients, wanting to do everything perfectly. This can be driven by a fear of losing the responsibility for these key areas, anxiety that others taking over will not be able to cope and occasionally the reverse – a fear that whoever takes over will outshine them so that they will be "found out". This can lead to an overzealous commitment to take a short leave and to stay connected with the business through e-mail and dialling into meetings. When noticing these behaviours we can explore what is driving them and, where necessary, challenge how realistic and authentic they are.

We should ensure we are supporting the individual and recognising where they are at. We may well need to give some reinforcing feedback and to be clear around our expectations of the individual at this time. If you feel the individual's emotions are significantly altered, you may want to seek support from HR or Occupational Health (go to page 82 to see more on the signs of pre-natal and post-natal depression).

**Top tips**

1. Be as open and transparent as possible and encourage open communication.

2. Give feedback to the individual about their value to the team.

3. Start discussions about how the individual sees their career and what they want.

4. Encourage others in the team to share their hopes and fears so these can be addressed openly.

## Coaching questions

1. How can you address your own hopes and fears to enable you to authentically support the individual with their feelings?

2. Ask – don't make assumptions about how people are feeling.

*"I think the hardest part is really pushing the support of the practice. Employees need to feel like we are going to back them and support what they need. My advice is really to make sure to work with your employees and those you are working with to make sure they are comfortable and have their needs covered."*
### Thomas Brown, Real Estate Partner, Ernst & Young

## The handover

Reinforcing the need for a properly planned and timely handover can help avoid serious problems later on for us, the team and the business. Involving the employee is an important step in the process and most individuals want to ensure an effective and timely handover as it can be the last thing people will remember of them for a while. Pregnant women in particular, do not want to find themselves stressed and working long hours in their final few weeks when they are less likely to have the energy.

We should start planning as soon as we know our team member is going off on leave. If we don't plan ahead, the handover is likely to be rushed and less effective. A poorly timed handover often leads to individuals working extreme hours. For those in the final trimester of pregnancy, this is the opposite of what should be happening to ensure their health and that of the baby. If we need cover, we should get the wheels in motion in the first few months after the announcement; it takes time to find internal or external resource and some individuals may need to leave earlier than expected.

If possible, give the individual permission to ramp down and pass work over earlier, not at the last minute. Encourage them to come up with ideas around how the role will be covered and to be actively involved in this process as it will help to make them feel valued.

With the employee, identify the component parts of their role and ask them to start writing handover notes if necessary. If covering the role internally consider which members of the team may thrive when given a stretch, as this could be a great development opportunity for them. If covering with other team members and the individual is planning to return to their role, it should be clear how they will get their work back. If external cover is needed, the job specification should be put together fast and budgetary approval signed off as soon as possible. Let the individual do the handover and, where relevant, ask for them to talk about how the work will be handed back. Although we may not be able to promise anything, we can share our intentions and make clear who is going to be accountable for what and from when. We can ask permission to connect with the leaver if there is an emergency and make sure we share the same view of an "emergency."

**Top tips**

1. Ensure internal and external clients are handled appropriately; where possible and particularly with key clients, get the individual going on leave to involve the person covering in final meetings or calls.

2. Make sure there is clarity around who will manage the team if their manager is going on leave.

3. Ensure the employee is involved and takes responsibility for the handover as well. They will have important insights into who is best placed to take on certain elements or clients.

4. Remember to manage individuals' fears about the completion of projects and what they will be coming back to.

5. Be mindful of individuals finding it hard to let go. This can be driven by guilt of letting their colleagues down or a fear of losing their professional identity.

6. Coach your colleague to start thinking about

what they will do when they are back and what the return might look like for them.

## Coaching questions

1.  What would a good handover look like for the individual, for you, for the business and for clients?

2.  What is going to get in the way of a good handover and how can you mitigate these factors?

# Managing adoption leave

Many of the tips for managing maternity and paternity leave similarly apply to managing an employee taking adoption leave. However, when a child is to be placed for adoption, the adopting parents may be advised only a short time beforehand. Therefore, although much of the general planning can take place, the exact timing is often unknown. We can support the employee and team to manage this uncertainty by preparing to manage their absence at short notice. We can also check our organisation's adoption policy as this might be different to the maternity policy in different geographies.

---

*Antenatal Appointments*
**During pregnancy, women need to attend important medical appointments and should be given the necessary time to attend these. It may be that the timings are inconvenient, but there is often a lack of flexibility from the health**

---

providers. In the UK, under current regulations, part-time employees are also entitled to time off for these appointments. They cannot be required to arrange them on non-working days. Bear this in mind on the lead up to a leave.

*"I found that help was provided by HR with the first couple of maternity leavers I managed, so this was positive. I recommend having open and full dialogue with the maternity leaver, and be aware of process and policies."*

**Manager, Professional Services Firm**

# 5

# Keeping in touch

## Before the maternity, paternity or adoption leave

It is vital to discuss with the individual how and what we are going to communicate while they are on leave. Everyone is different so it's important to have a conversation around their expectations and what they want. Remember what they think they want before they go may change whilst they are on leave, so during this time check in with them and see if their needs have changed. We will also need to manage their expectations if what they are asking for feels like it will not be possible. Who else could they get information from? It may be difficult if we promise something and then do not deliver, as this can break trust.

Typically individuals want little communication in the first few months and then increase the amount of connection slowly with most of the re-engagement two to three months before they return. Those who keep in touch whilst they are on leave can find it easier to understand what has happened in the meantime. This can also help make the reintegration smoother, so it is a good idea to engage with individuals whilst they are off.

Discuss how bonuses, pay rises, appraisals and promotions will be handled while they are away. To capture the most recent deliverables, individuals may appreciate a performance review prior to their leave. This can help to manage expectations about pay and, where relevant, bonuses. This will also give us an opportunity to talk about future career plans in the medium term, which can provide affirmation around career momentum.

**Top tips**

1.  Liaise with HR colleagues to discuss any specific requirements.

2.  Don't be afraid to have conversations to discuss expectations.

3.  You may explain that the more notice they can give of their return date, the better able you will be to plan a smooth re-integration for them.

4.  Agree with the individual how to stay connected during their leave, to help build confidence and engagement on their return.

**Coaching questions**

1.  What do they want to be kept informed of? How do they want to communicate; by email, telephone or meeting up? How often do they want to hear from the office? Do they want others on the team to also be in touch?

2.  What would you want to know about if you were out of the business for a period of time?

3.  What expectations would you have of your colleagues around keeping in touch?

4.  Are you clear about what communication you have committed to and how you can fulfil this?

*"My employee is on maternity leave at the moment and my tips for managing the leave would be:*

*1. Establish the expected pattern of communication before your employee goes on maternity leave (i.e. preferred frequency, regularity, medium, types of info they'd like to hear about, etc).*

*2. Listen and react to their needs; be flexible and accommodating to the extent possible, rather than making assumptions based on your own experience, even if that is personal experience of maternity leave or your partner having maternity leave – your employee may have a very different view and needs."*

**Manager, Financial Services Firm**

# SECTION 3:

## On leave

# 6

# Managing maternity, paternity or adoption leave

*Summary:*
Whilst your employee is on leave they will still be thinking about work, their career and what they are coming back to. There can be a feeling of *"out of sight, out of mind"*, but it is vitally important that you contact the individual as planned. Regular communication on leave can help the individual re-integrate quicker. Think through the return and how to make it a success and discuss this with the individual before they are back at work.

In the previous chapter we talked about the agreed communication plan for leave, who the employee will stay connected with and how. We need to make sure that we schedule and follow through on our commitments.

It is sometimes difficult for future mothers and fathers to be clear about what a significant shift in identity becoming a parent for the first time is. Remember that sometimes the perception of how frequently they want to be in touch with the business when on leave and the reality once their child arrives may be different. It is a good idea to re-contract what we have agreed with our colleague a few months after the start of their leave because their expectations could have changed.

We should be clear and concise about what we want to communicate to our colleague when we speak to them. We can put ourselves in their shoes and think about what is important to them, for example; changes in the organisation, team, business, major projects completed, key strategic changes or new business won. It can be helpful to stay with the bigger picture and ask if they want more detail.

We need to plan for our team, achieving objectives and to make sure there is a smooth return. So, if we want to discuss planned return dates, we should have the conversation during a scheduled catch up. It is fine to ask the question around timeframes but don't put pressure on the individual to be definite about their plans, there is a lot of change for them and it might take them time to know how they feel.

It can be useful for us to find out what their thoughts are (i.e. if they want to come back part-time or flexibly) so we can think about whether we will be able to accommodate any changes. Think about when they have indicated they will return and remember they may not be ready to discuss their return in the early days or months of maternity.

On a practical note, things like organising childcare, weaning or sleep deprivation might impact on when the best time is for them to come back and perform optimally.

Given how quickly organisations change and the length of leave, many employees have new line managers when they return to work. It is important, if we are taking over as a new line manager that we prepare for the return even more fully. This is the first interaction we may have with our new colleague so we will want to make a good first impression and get the best response from them too. Try and connect with them a couple of months before they come back.

*"Put yourself in their shoes, don't try to assume what you think they feel or want, be fair."*

**Manager, Professional Services Firm**

---

*KIT DAYS*

**While your colleague is still on leave, in the UK, you can suggest using Keeping in Touch (KIT) days to help them reconnect and get back up to speed. Under UK Law, since 2007 employees may agree to work for up to 10 days during their maternity leave. These KIT days are generally paid at basic salary rate and must be planned and arranged by mutual agreement. Sometimes individuals want to use them to attend key client meetings, team away days or strategy days, and to get reacquainted with policies, procedures and technology. They also provide an opportunity to participate in any training. KIT days can be combined with social events, allowing individuals to catch up with evolving team dynamics. Some people simply appreciate the opportunity to get back in touch with their professional identity, putting on the work clothes, practising the commute and stepping back into their office environment. Our clients often mention how useful KIT days have been in rebuilding their confidence or phasing back into their roles.**

---

## Returner's checklist

We will normally know well in advance when the individual is returning. At this stage we will need to think about any applications for flexible working and get clarity around the role the individual is returning to.

As soon as we do know the return date there are a number of things that we can start to think through with the employee and the extended team.

## Top tips

1. Unless otherwise agreed, individuals generally return to their original role. Check with HR if you are unsure about this: the individual will want clarity around what they are coming back to.

2. What does their role look like now – does their original role still exist? Is it what they want to come back to? Does it fit with their intended working pattern or style?

3. Make sure you talk through how clients and key projects can be handed back to ensure continuity of career for the returner.

4. Think about reading material or short development courses that could help get an individual back up to speed.

5. Have any systems or technical aspects of their role changed, and would some training or

mentoring help?

6. Think about the possibility of phased returns so that people have the choice of gradually easing back into the workplace.

7. Make sure the practical things are sorted out – desk, computer, passes, car parking, pay and benefits, etc. There is nothing worse than coming back to chaos on this front and it sends a poor message about how well planned the return is.

8. Help colleagues prepare for the reintegration of their team member. If the team has changed think of how you can plan a team event or day to help them bond and adjust to the returner.

9. If you are a new line manager, make sure you spend some time reviewing the individual's previous performance reviews, career development plans and speaking to stakeholders who know your returner.

10. Prepare yourself for conversations around flexible working and start considering what may be possible in your team and in the individual's role – if you have questions, ask for the advice and support of HR.

11. Communicate with the individual around any changes.

12. Communicate return plans to the team.

## Coaching questions

1. What are your key concerns while the individual is on leave?

2. What can you learn from this experience?

3. If you take on managing someone already on leave, how can you build the relationship in order to make the return smoother?

4. How could your team member make best use of keeping in touch?

5. Think about who else it would be helpful for your colleague to connect with prior to their return?

6. What more could you do to pre-empt any challenges they may face on their return?

# SECTION 4:

## Back to work

# 7

# Managing the reintegration

*Summary:*
The return to work after maternity, paternity or adoption leave can be akin to starting a new position. It needs to be actively and positively managed. Identify all the changes which have occurred and explore what flexible work patterns can be offered. Create a re-induction plan with the individual for the first days, weeks and months – a 100 day plan can work wonders.

Individuals are often excited about their return to work and can't wait to get back. They are motivated by using their intellect and being able to achieve meaningful deliverables. The opportunity to re-engage with their colleagues and to have time to do something for themselves are really positive aspects of going back to work for many. Despite this, returning from an extended leave can be a daunting task.

Organisations can change very rapidly. Individuals may be coming back to a vastly different environment or business model, and quite often a changed team or new line manager. They may well be energised about getting back to work but may also face the challenges of getting back up to speed with new systems, processes, information and knowledge. These factors combined with establishing new routines and their identity as a working parent makes it a significant transition to navigate.

For some, having an extended period of time out can impact heavily on confidence levels. This and the change in demands on the individual outside of work can lead to challenges around the way they work. It can also put into question what a successful professional is in their eyes. The changes and extra demands or constraints can lead to guilt and can trigger stress in working parents whose focus has previously been on their career and who have had significant career momentum. As a manager we will need to watch out for changes in confidence and give the individual feedback regularly. This will help them to get over any initial nerves and confidence issues quicker.

The stereotypes and unconscious biases around the perceived changes in commitment and expectations of a working parent may add to the pressure they feel. Sometimes working parents feel that they have a different capacity than they used to, because they need to navigate different boundaries and expectations. Since they are unable to work the way they used to, they can feel less confident in their position in the work place. This realignment in identity is not to be confused with a lack of ambition, drive and desire to maintain career momentum, which for many remains crucial. During these adjustments, self-doubt can creep in. Individuals at this time will generally respond best to a supportive, encouraging management style. Setting clear expectations and providing regular feedback may help to rebuild confidence more quickly.

If we want individuals in our team to be successful and to perform well, it is important to understand the commitments they have and how best to get high productivity from them in the time they have available. In Chapter 8 we look in more detail about how to approach requests for flexible working arrangements, which may support this.

Let the team know the date of the individual's return and any agreed flexible arrangements. Consider how to welcome the employee back into the team and make sure that they have a desk and computer set up for their first day back. Discuss the handing back of responsibilities, projects and clients, and support them in making this happen. Arrange for them to get to know new team members. In particular, address any potential conflicts of interest or overlaps in role before they become difficult to manage. Encourage the individual to discuss their new working pattern with the team.

**Top tips**

1. Work with the individual to agree a sustainable flexible working arrangement, if appropriate.

2. Create a re-induction plan.

3. Ensure that passes, passwords, IT and other technology are up to date and working for their return.

4. Make sure you meet with them the day they return.

5.  Plan to catch up regularly in the first few months back.

6.  Inform team and give feedback on changes to working patterns.

7.  Make sure that you are giving the right messages of support to the team and business.

8.  Be mindful that there **may** be issues around guilt or self-confidence, but don't assume this will be the case.

9.  Suspend judgment for a while. The early weeks can be challenging for the returner, some may take longer than others to adjust to the return to work.

10. Set clear expectations and agree some early milestones.

11. Keep talking.


**Coaching questions**

1.  What will a successful return in this case look and feel like for you, the individual and the team?

2.  What creative flexible working options can you offer? Where can the role be flexible and where can't it?

3. How and when will you know if the return has been successful?

4. What team dynamics might cause difficulties or make the return easier?

5. How can you collectively work together to make the reintegration a success? (Take a look at the following section for more guidance.)

*"I have one person I am managing through leave and am 32 weeks pregnant myself so I have first-hand experience! The firm has been nothing but positive, but I have learnt valuable lessons with my team member around the importance of the Partners investing time in ensuring the right resourcing decisions were made for her. We didn't get it right and this is something we are doing differently next time round. Remember that no one size fits all, so open and honest communication and giving permission are the most helpful things we can do."*

**Kate Bamford, Manager, Professional Services Firm**

## Managing the team for success

As with any other management task it is worthwhile thinking through the objectives and measures of success for a smooth reintegration back, especially when the employee is returning to an alternative work pattern.

As with any addition to a team, the return of the individual will shift the dynamics. It can be helpful to get the team to think through how it will be, how they can best help to reintegrate their colleague, and the roles they can take. As the manager it is important to think about how the dynamics may shift – will there be winners and losers following the return? Will some people be resistant or too keen to hand back the responsibilities and clients they have been given and how can we best manage that? What conversations do we need to have and what should we encourage the individual to discuss with the team?

If there are tensions we will need to make a decision

about what we expect and proactively manage this. For example if someone's role has been split across a couple of team members and they have risen to the challenge, we need to think about how they might continue to be developed and motivated. Have conversations with the individual coming back around what they want. This could be an opportunity to redefine the role and to enable the individual to step up a gear and take on more of a leadership position or to relinquish bits of their role in order to be able to work part-time. If we are expecting them to move up it might be important to support them or get coaching support for them in this shift.

We will need to help support the reintegration process and look out for individuals in the business who are consciously or unconsciously making it difficult. It may be necessary to sit down and talk to them about what is going on and what their expectations of the individual's return are.

As with any other management task and team adjustment, this transition requires the collective to assess how well the objectives we set are being met. We could spend part of our team meetings talking through how the reintegration is going, what is working, what could be done better and who is accountable for improving it. This will be particularly important if we have a colleague returning to work in a more flexible capacity – what is working well with the chosen work pattern and the team dynamics; what may be having a detrimental impact on that team and needs to be adjusted?

Checking in with individuals to test the mood and gain

insights prior to team meetings will be beneficial and the importance of having one to one time with the returner at regular intervals cannot be overstated. This will help us to understand how well he or she is reintegrating, will help us build their confidence and deal with any issue that may arise in a timely way.

Remember to encourage the team to be open about how they are working and what their needs are. If one individual is working very differently, frustrations may emerge, so it is good to get all the team to share their thoughts and expectations, and how they would like to work.

**Some suggested measures of success**

1. The returner has access to the building, networks, a desk, computer, etc.

2. The returner has the right pay and benefits on their return.

3. The rapidity with which the returner gets back up to speed with changes in knowledge, policy, and practice to perform their role.

4. The performance of the team and business in the months after the return.

5. The performance of the returner in the first 6 months following the return.

6. The ability of the team to openly communicate through challenges.

7.  The ability of the team to celebrate success and give each other positive feedback.

8.  The returner has "meaningful" work soon after their return.

9.  Clients and projects have been successfully handed over.

10. The team's engagement and satisfaction levels are high.

11. Alternative work patterns have been a success.

# Managing flexible working – helping colleagues and the team find their balance

*Summary:*
It's important to have a rounded view of the circumstances when considering the implementation of flexible working. Make sure you understand what the boundaries are for the individual, the potential challenges and what will help to make it work. Be open minded and think about creative ways to implement flexibility.

Some working parents have constraints around their working day as a result of childcare provision and a desire to spend quality time with their children. This might mean agreeing a part-time working pattern, for others it might mean leaving at 5pm and picking their child up from nursery or a child minder, or relieving their nanny. For others it might be logging-in in the evenings or working from home some days.

Dual-career families will have the additional challenge of juggling two busy diaries to make the week work and ensure their child or children are well looked after.

As a manager it is useful for us to understand our employee's plans, what they can do and what their particular constraints are, if they have any. When can they be flexible and when can't they? It is good to know what their boundaries are and to help them shape these in a way that is realistic for the job they are doing. There is no point agreeing to a flexible working pattern which will mean they can't succeed in their job. For example, if they need to talk to people in the US regularly and want to leave at 5pm to pick up their child every day, but are not prepared to do anything later in the evening from home, this could be a real challenge to delivering their objectives. However, if they are happy to make calls after their children are in bed, this could work really very well.

We should consider how our agreement with them impacts on the rest of the team and discuss this with them. Ask the individual about how they are going to work with the team; make sure they understand the potential challenges and get them to think about ways these can be overcome.

It may also mean that others have a chance to work in a slightly different way. For instance, if the working parent wants to come in early and leave at 5.30pm, someone else may want to come in later and work later. If we want individuals in our team to be successful and to perform well, it is crucial to understand the commitments they have and how best to get high productivity from them in the time they have available.

**Top tips**

1.  Get HR involved early in flexible working discussions and agreements.

2. Think through the role the individual has and what types of flexibility may be best suited.

3. Consider what you have seen work well in the past.

4. Given the team you have, are there adjustments that may need to be made?

5. Assess how many of the team are currently working flexibly – what impact will another flexible worker have?

6. Think through what is possible as opposed to what you don't want to happen – frame the challenge positively.

7. Be commercial about the decision you are making; be clear as to what will work and what you think may be a challenge.

8. Ask for others' opinions to make sure you see other points of view.

9. Be clear that flexibility is a two way street and that it works best when it isn't too rigid.

10. Set realistic boundaries and expectations from the start and manage them.

11. Be creative and trial new or different ways of working.

12. Specify a time for a trial period and agree in advance how you will measure the success of the

arrangements. Have regular check-ins to assess progress, nip any issues in the bud and fine tune the arrangement.

## Coaching questions

1.  What are you trying to achieve through offering flexibility?

2.  How can you and the individual ensure they have a flexible work load appropriate to their flexible work pattern?

3.  How sustainable is the arrangement? When are you going to review it?

4.  If you work in a long–hours culture, where people regularly exceed their contracted hours, how will this impact the implementation of any flexible arrangement? What are the unwritten assumptions about working beyond contracted hours? How can you accommodate this in the arrangement?

5.  If you already have someone working flexibly, how can this be better? What can you do to optimise the arrangement?

6.  What are your concerns? And your team's concerns? What might other stakeholders' concerns be? How can you overcome them?

*"My experience has been very positive. There is a high rate of maternity returners in our office because the piece around flexible working is well managed and also there is a belief that there is an inherent fairness in the process. It's important to never make assumptions about how people are feeling."*

**Manager, Professional Services Firm**

# 9

# Managing sickness and absences

**Summary:**
**This section looks at the challenges of managing sickness and absence which can be common when working with employees who have young children. Often when children are young and first go to nursery they catch lots of viruses – if your employee doesn't have family or support around them this can create logistical challenges.**

It is essential to recognise that our employees with children have caring responsibilities. Although someone is employed full-time, once they are a parent they will have responsibility 24 hours, 7 days a week for their child even if they are physically not with them. This means that although they are working professionals, they have ultimate responsibility for another human being, which will at times need to come first.

Check your company policy, is there any provision for individuals with caring responsibilities? Although there are statutory requirements to support employees when they are sick, and to have limited unpaid leave to look after a sick child, your company may or may not have a policy on supporting employees when their dependents are sick.

Having a child off sick is one of the most frustrating and stressful elements for a working parent, particularly in the early days. Young children do pick up lots of illnesses and many childcare providers do not take sick children into care. Most families no longer have the social fabric that previous generations enjoyed, so they may not have the support of family locally or a community they know well. This means that when their normal childcare solution falls down it can be hard to find back up.

If we have an employee who seems to be taking time off for their own sickness, and their child's, start the conversations early about what is going on and how they are coping. The earlier we have informal conversations the easier it will be to understand what the challenge is. Ask open questions, empathise and see what support they need to help them manage better.

Remember, most employees will find managing time off as a result of a child's sickness very stressful and it can lead to guilt especially as it is normally unforeseen. They will be acutely aware of the impact it is having. They will have conflicting feelings of wanting to be with their sick child and caring for them, and wanting to do a good job and not to let others down.

In extreme cases the guilt can lead to internal doubt and concerns about how sustainable the status quo is and potentially, in some cases whether they should give up work. It is beneficial to have conversations with the individual so they feel understood, motivated, supported and able to see a way through this challenging time. There may be some instances where we give some informal allowance to individuals who are struggling with a dependant's sickness.

Whatever we do, we should be transparent about why we are making allowances and be consistent. We cannot be seen to be treating people differently or to be positively discriminating. Equally, if we are not supportive, the individual may feel pressured and highly conflicted, which could impact on their performance and long term engagement with the business.

Talk to the team and manage the policy. If you are concerned about the sickness or absence of your employee, talk to HR. Repeated time off for sickness may also be indicative of an employee struggling with an unsustainable work load or work pattern.

**Top tips**

1.  Talk early about sickness and absence before it becomes an issue.

2.  Be clear and consistent about how you manage working parents through this.

3.  Understand what is going on and what the challenges are.

4.  Are there issues in their working pattern and would a different pattern work better?

5.  Be empathetic – most employees find these absences stressful too.

6.  Make sure the individual knows you are aware and understand what is going on.

6.  Manage the team's perceptions and help the individual to maintain positive relationships.

## Coaching questions

1.  What are your underlying concerns about the returner's absences?

2.  What unconscious biases could impact how you manage the absences?

3.  What can you do to maintain the team performance in the short term and in the medium term?

*"I have managed approximately 10 leaves in total in the last 18 months; I think it's important to attend any courses or coaching, but also seek legal advice."*
**Manager, Finance Industry**

# 10

# Career conversations

**Summary:**
For most professionals who are having a child, a primary consideration is: *what will happen to my career and what do I want from my career?* There are likely to be challenges and questions they are asking themselves. Make sure you ask them what they want and don't make assumptions.

For some, becoming a working parent does mean priorities shift, but it doesn't necessarily mean that individuals are less committed to their careers. It is a significant element of their identity and purpose, and they have achieved great things. However, many people may have to approach their careers in different ways and this usually means looking for more flexibility. This can come in various ways.

For many people, flexibility will be informal shifts in their working week or working day – starting earlier, leaving earlier, logging back on at night. For others there is the formal request to work in a flexible capacity, which we covered in chapter 8.

Many individuals have spent a long time building up their careers before they start a family. A career is often a very important part of these individuals, but having a family can add additional commitments and a new identity. To better understand how to retain and support individuals returning after having a family it is important to discuss their career with them. Find out what they want now and how they want to plan their future. Discuss realistic options based on their requirements and the business needs. The more open we can both be the more likely we are to come up with a positive, achievable solution.

During this transition, many professionals need to reflect on and address the challenges around the shape of their careers, and the speed at which they want to progress. Once again, be careful not to make assumptions. Someone who has had a child may want to accelerate or slow their career progression. For many this is not a choice, particularly if they are the main breadwinner. For other professionals career advancement will remain crucial to their engagement and satisfaction with work. However, some working parents will want to find a balance. They may need to explore the trade-offs between the hours they are willing to work and the speed at which their career progresses.

Organisations offering flexibility in career models and patterns are better placed to engage with employees who have significant responsibilities outside of work, such as caring for children and older relatives. There is often a disconnect between the organisation's stated approach and what happens in practice. This is where the role of the line manager can be crucial in exploring options and providing support to create sustainable careers for valued professionals.

As there are a wide range of expectations for working parents, the line manager needs to create the space for meaningful conversations about career progression and aspirations. We can have an honest dialogue with our colleague about our own expectations, as well as theirs, and how best to realise them. This may require us to adopt a coaching approach to explore options. Although some individuals may choose a flatter career trajectory for the time being, many find it difficult to manage their own expectations and fears. For high achievers it can be tough to see colleagues' careers accelerate faster than their own, even when they have made a conscious decision to slow down.

The timing of these discussions is important. Once the individual has some experience of life as a working parent, they will have a clearer sense of what some of the challenges may be for them. However, if the conversation is delayed too long, they may feel we are no longer interested or they don't have any options.

Most working parents are very much in "survival" mode when they first return from leave. There are many moving parts which they need to get their heads around and it takes time to establish what works and what doesn't. It is important for the line manager to give them time and space to see the larger perspective and to help them work out short and midterm career plans. When this support is provided, the individual can move from survival mode to finding a sustainable approach to their career. Sometimes this will require small adjustments to the role in order to make it more compatible with caring responsibilities. Helping colleagues identify and learn from role models can also be very empowering for them.

**Top tips**

1. Support the individual to make a clear assessment of what career options are feasible.

2. Be clear on what your organisation's perspective is on career flexibility.

3. Make sure you have timely conversations on careers after your colleague returns.

4. Continue the career dialogue through the first year because perspectives may change.

5. Make sure you are creating a safe and open environment to have an honest dialogue. It is important you agree job and career design and are aligned on expectations.

6. Notice and challenge your own assumptions. Individuals have varying hopes, aspirations and circumstances.

**Coaching questions**

1. How would you describe the culture in your part of the organisation? Is there an expectation professionals will continue to move up or move out?

2. How does the culture differ elsewhere in the organisation?

3. What opportunities are there for shifting the norms to create flexibility in career patterns?

4. How can you influence the culture in your area?

# 11

# Feedback

*Summary:*
**Providing feedback enables the individual to understand clearly what others expect of them. You should also consider what expectations they are placing on themselves. Set up regular opportunities for feedback conversations.**

Giving and receiving feedback is a vital ingredient in managing a smooth transition. Our role is to encourage high quality work, while fostering an environment of clarity about what is expected and about how individuals are performing. By enabling people to give each other feedback, we ensure any questions or concerns are dealt with before they become problematic.

Many parents returning to work after having children find one of the fundamental challenges is around what they think others expect and, more importantly, what they expect of themselves. As a line manager, we can make sure the individual understands what is expected of them, when they need to deliver and to what extent they are meeting expectations. Consider what the key deliverables are in their job. We may also offer constructive feedback on the individual's working style, impact and added value.

**Top tips**

1.   Give frequent and regular constructive feedback.

2.   Don't be afraid to give feedback. Often people know what you are going to tell them and are relieved to discuss it.

3.   Give specific and descriptive feedback around positive and challenging behaviours, including their impact, and suggestions of what could be different.

4.   Give feedback on behaviours not personality.

5.   Help to think through other ways of doing things. Provide ideas about what could work even better.

6.   Set clear and realistic expectations.

7.   Measure feedback on deliverables not presenteeism.

8.   Look out for people who are working in an extreme way to demonstrate becoming a parent has made no difference to their commitment levels. Explore if this is what they want or if it is driven by a fear of being written off. Be aware of engagement levels throughout the first year.

9.   Regularly discuss feedback on whether expectations are being met on both sides.

10. Involve other team members in discussions so solutions and accountabilities can be collectively agreed. Monitor the group dynamics.

11. Provide support and stretch. Some mothers and fathers will lack confidence when they return and will need extra help to realise what is possible.

## Coaching questions

1. What might get in the way of you giving the individual the feedback they need?

2. How have you felt after you have been given feedback?

3. What benefit is there in giving the feedback you want to give?

# Additional considerations

# 12

# Reward and recognition

**Summary:**
Proper management of an individual's review, and what they're expecting from it, is never more important than before and after that person's extended leave. Clarity and consistency are key to making this process a constructive element of their transition. Use this as a prompt to make sure you are as informed as possible about your company's policies in this area, and how you should be implementing them.

Reward and recognition are basic motivators for most people. One of the key reasons people go back to work is for financial independence or to fulfil a current lifestyle they have. They may also be thinking about achieving the things they want for their family, for example affording the right environment and schooling.

Reward and recognition are often highly emotional topics for individuals and if managed poorly can change the individuals' confidence as well as commitment to the organisation.

Discussing the individuals' performance with them before they go on leave can be very useful. It will help them to be clear about how they are doing beforehand. Most organisations have policies around how to rank individuals who have had periods of time out. It is vital to check these policies and make sure that we are consistent in the way we rank individuals on maternity, adoption or paternity leave. Seek advice from HR if the policy does not seem clear. If we think there are going to be unusually high or low bonuses, or the individual is likely to get less than previously expected because of performance, it can be useful to make sure we are managing their expectations early on.

Where there is a mismatch in expectations, and individuals get a shock when they are on leave, people can feel they are not valued and are being treated differently due to their leave. This can lead to deep feelings of resentment and a decision to leave the organisation.

If you are unclear how to deal with an individual's rating, pay, promotion or bonus, seek advice from HR; it is better to get it right and to be consistent. Similarly, for those returning on flexible working arrangements, consider what they need to do in order to meet and exceed expectations. Base this on a realistic assessment of the outputs someone will be able to achieve in the time that they are there i.e. a 60% person shouldn't be measured against being 100%.

**Top tips**

1.  Early in the process, discuss with colleagues and the individual how the reward policies apply in practice.

2.  Agree how reward and recognition will be communicated on leave.

3. Conduct a mini performance review before the individual goes on leave.

4. If you are not ultimately responsible for deciding reward and recognition, speak to those who are.

5. Establish what is expected of the returner and what can they expect in recognition of the work they have done.

6. Discuss any concerns with HR.

## Coaching questions

1. How confident are you in managing the appraisals, advancement and bonuses of those on maternity, paternity or adoptive leave and those returning?

2. What seems fair to you? How does this fit with the organisation's and individual's expectations?

3. What discretion can you exercise to reward their achievements?

4. What do you think their expectations are and why?

# 13

# The extended team

*Summary:*
An important area of concern when managing maternity, paternity, or adoption leave is the impact on the wider team. There can be many different aspects and dynamics to a team, all of which can be affected by time out or a change in the working patterns of one employee. Be sure to communicate regularly with all concerned, to avoid any uncertainty that might put undue pressure on how they all work together.

As a manager we are focussed on making sure strategy is delivered and creating a high performing team which accomplishes their objectives. This means paying attention to the wellbeing of all members of the team and really understanding what they all want from work and life. Everyone will be different and will have different desires and outcomes so these need to be explored without making assumptions.

The team may be split between working parents and non-parents, which can create a range of different dynamics. It is often difficult for people without children to truly understand the challenges of having a young family. The impact of continuous nights with broken sleep and new commitments outside of work can be hard to comprehend unless we have experienced it.

One of the key areas of focus when managing

working parents is making sure the team is happy and supportive of any adjustments to working patterns. It is also important that they do not feel short changed as a result of parents' childcare demands.

Try to take a holistic view of the deliverables and how accountabilities are split; ensure each team member is clear on their required outputs and outcomes, and how best to work together to meet these objectives. The focus on outputs and outcomes is very important here. Many of the working parents that we coach work unusual patterns – maybe operating a 9-6 working day in the office but then logging back in to complete key tasks or respond to email traffic.

The make-up of every team is very different. Some managers will have a whole team of working parents, while others will just have one. The challenges and group think for those teams therefore vary. As a manager it is vital to get the team to communicate effectively about workload, objectives and outcomes, as well as people's preferences in working style and patterns. Managers need to be both supportive of alternatives but also challenging if they are not going to help the team deliver its objectives. We also need to avoid being overly biased toward one group or another – which in turn requires an awareness of our own limiting beliefs about flexible working.

When we are managing a working parent who takes time out to have or look after a child it can be more difficult to plan and deal with workflow for the entire team, especially in challenging economic conditions. In order to avoid uncertainty, it is important to plan ahead as much as we can and keep the team updated (with the consent of the individual) as soon as we know what is happening.

Successful management of a team with flexible workers requires the manager to create an environment where the team members can openly discuss what is working, the challenges that need addressing and what needs to change to find the correct balance. Of course this is not static either, as people's circumstances change and members leave or join the team. We can try to think creatively and make sure we have enough resource for the team to be able to function effectively.

The team working well together is critical to their performance and the success of the business. It can be useful to have some agreements which allow people to work in the way that suits them. If someone likes sending emails at 10pm at night make sure you make it clear that others are not expected to respond at this time. Be clear and discuss how you like to work so others understand.

**Top tips**

1. Think about who is in your team? What is the split of working parents and non parents? How do they function together and what works well?

2. Think about the nature of your work and the type of commitment it requires?

3. What might some of the challenges be for working parents? Get your team to brainstorm solutions.

4. How can you make it equitable for everyone?

5. Talk to individual team members to get their views and ideas.

6. Set some clear values and behaviours for the team; act as a role model and set the tone for how your team work together and how they support working parents.

7. Encourage team members to talk to each other and find out what is important to them. Get working parents to share their challenges and non parents to discuss what they want.

**Coaching questions**

1. What are you trying to achieve with your team?

2. How can you build and maintain a team of diverse people, who will work well towards this purpose?

3. What behaviours are you going to recognise and reward?

*"My experience managing maternity has been good. We have a high proportion of mothers (and fathers) working flexibly in the team and this has created a positive atmosphere about maternity or paternity leave and the need to positively reintroduce the team member back. We are always resource constrained so there is little slack in the team to take up the extra work."*

**Manager, Financial Services Firm**

# 14

# Handling some difficult situations

*Summary:*
Becoming a parent can be a source of much uncertainty and change in a colleague's life. It's important as a manager to be aware of this and to manage any changes in a positive and supportive way. Communication is vital at sensitive times; tackle issues as soon as they arise, before they become problematic.

Remember that these situations don't occur every day. As a manager it is good to understand what help there is in the organisation to support the individual if they do find themselves in one of these scenarios. It is also important for us to be clear around what our role as their manager is in this and to make sure that we are communicating effectively.

## Miscarriages

Sadly some pregnancies do not go their full term and when a colleague has a miscarriage it is critical to recognise that this can be a very upsetting and sometimes traumatic event. We can give them space and time out of work to reflect and grieve. Inform the team, with the permission of your colleague, so that they too can be aware and sensitive to the situation. Communicate regularly with the individual.

## Pre or Post natal depression

Depression can occur during pregnancy or after the birth. Some estimate that as many as 70% of women will experience symptoms of depression during pregnancy, making it a widespread concern. However, these depressive symptoms are often more minor than a full blown diagnostic depression, which is typically only seen in about 10-15% of pregnant women.

While hormones are often blamed for many of the mood swings, and other emotional and psychological happenings in pregnancy, they are only one part of the picture when it comes to pregnancy and depression. Sometimes the stress of pregnancy brings on depressive symptoms, even when the pregnancy was planned. These feelings might intensify if the pregnancy is complicated, unplanned, or if there are broader sources of intense stress, such as moving house to accommodate a larger family or work related issues.

More serious depression in pregnancy can have a negative impact on good prenatal care, particularly in the areas of nutrition, sleep habits, exercise and following care instructions from the doctor or midwife. This in turn can have an obvious impact on health and wellbeing, and consequently work.

Many of the signs of depression mimic pregnancy symptoms. It can be hard to determine what normal fatigue in pregnancy is and what depression is. If someone is suffering from excessive fatigue it is really crucial that they seek some professional advice. There can be a tendency to ignore depression in pregnancy simply because this is supposed to be a happy time in life; this includes the pregnant woman herself. Here are some of the signs or symptoms:

- Problems concentrating
- Problems with sleeping
- Fatigue
- Changes in eating habits
- Feeling anxious
- Irritability
- Feeling blue

The key to preventing problems that stem from depression in pregnancy, which may also increase the likelihood of postpartum depression, is getting timely support. If we realise that a colleague is experiencing problems we can help them find appropriate support through the right channels. We can offer support through recognising that they are not alone and that help is available.

**Check whether your organisation has an Employee Assistance Programme or an Occupational Health adviser, and encourage the individual to seek help from their doctor. It is useful to be aware of what support your organisation can offer.**

## Performance issues

It is really important to address performance issues in a timely way, before they become a problem. However, when someone's pregnant we should also be mindful of how we manage this as the performance issue may be related to their pregnancy. Gain clarity around what the reason for the performance issue is and support the colleague in seeking a solution. Discuss the issues with the individual. Seek advice from HR about how best to handle the scenario.

Because there are so many elements to the transition, the ability to understand why there are performance issues and supporting our colleague in finding a solution is critical. It may well be that the performance issues can be rectified very quickly through practical changes.

## Maternity cover that was good

Sometimes we may feel that the person covering the leave has performed really well, brought different skills to the role, and the team is in a really good place. Having to reintegrate the returning employee can feel unsettling, and can leave us feeling frustrated at another disruption and change to the current team dynamic, which could be working well. It can also make us feel less enthusiastic about the return of the individual than we thought we would be. We need to try to be in the best mindset before they are back at work. It is good to think through the benefits of the individual returning. Is there scope for another team member? Is there a way to structure the team differently to play to the strengths of the individual returning? Remember to talk to HR as there are statutory requirements to consider.

It may well be that the individual returning feels

threatened by the person who has covered and done a good job. This could impact their confidence on return and make them feel unsettled. It is therefore important that we, as the manager, try to be objective and support the individual on their return.

It may be that we feel there are areas for development and we can coach the individual on their return around how to best manage this. Do this slowly and be sensitive to their confidence levels.

Remember different people have different styles; it may be that other working patterns or models may work.

## Self confidence

We have referred to confidence levels at a number of stages throughout the book. As a manager we can help reinforce the value of our colleague and, where the opportunities arise, to recognise where good work has been delivered. This can be particularly important in the initial months after the return from leave, which can be a period of great uncertainty and change.

It is well documented that one of the challenges for working parents is that they often feel like they are not delivering well on any core aspect of their life – they are finding it hard to deliver as the professional they were and are struggling to be the parent that they want to be because of career commitments.

Positive affirmation of a strong return and work done

as it is delivered can make a huge impact on how confident and engaged a returner will be. It is a virtuous circle.

The opposite can be very detrimental to confidence, performance and engagement. A negative spiral can easily unravel. It can be useful to provide coaching to support individuals in developing their confidence on their return. Give people a bit of slack when they return; they will need time to get up to speed.

## Guilt

This is the bane of all working parents' lives. Guilt is driven from a sense of letting a third party down; not being there for the children, having to leave work before everyone else, not being able to take clients out as often in the evenings, not finding enough time for a partner, and so on.

At its most extreme guilt can manifest itself in a feeling that you are not being true to your authentic self – the image you had of being a working parent is not unfolding in the way you wanted or expected. It is at this point that generally something has to shift and it often results in individuals leaving. This is why it is so important for line managers to communicate effectively and have regular meetings, both informal and formal, in order to manage issues before they become insurmountable. Coaching can help people to get the right success measures so guilt isn't overwhelming.

## Managing clients' expectations

One of the biggest fears for managers can be the impact the leave will have on internal or external clients who are expecting the delivery of a product, service or project to continue.

Similarly if the employee returns and requests to work flexibly we need to consider how best to position this with existing and new clients. In our experience there is often a misguided fear that clients will immediately take their business elsewhere, which often couldn't be further from the truth.

Remember, many clients are working parents themselves and in a lot of cases the event can act as a means of connecting with clients on a different level. If a client values your relationship they are not going to leave by virtue of the fact a colleague has gone on leave or is working flexibly.

It is best to be realistic about fears and to instead manage them through effective consultation with the client. They will feel far more respected if this is managed well and it could help build a different and deeper connection on a more personal and human level.

## Managing the returner's expectations

As we have seen, some of the common challenges facing teams with working parents are the unexpected absences due to children's illness or a breakdown in childcare. On this topic we should help colleagues think through the back up that they have planned in case primary childcare does break down; some organisations will pay for emergency childcare provision.

We can make sure that challenges and frictions within the team regarding working patterns or the allocation of work are dealt with in a timely way before they become a problem. This again requires team members to openly communicate frustrations or issues as they arise.

In addition, it is critical that those with alternative working patterns take accountability for minimising the impact that this can have on the team, as well as other stakeholders. Equally, it is good to recognise the challenges working parents may face.

### Top tips

1.  Address issues as they arise, before they become tough to manage.

2. Ask don't assume.

3. Listen well.

4. Be courageous, creative and commercial.

5. Seek wise counsel.

## Coaching questions

1. What is your best hope for this transition?

2. What is your worst fear?

3. What is in your control?

4. What do you need to feel confident and competent as a manager of a working parent?

5. What further support do you want and where can you get this?

6. What can you do now?

# Conclusions

As a manager, maternity, paternity or adoption transitions can be extremely easy or extremely challenging to manage. Even though someone might have a good pregnancy and goes on leave on a great note, there can be issues that arise subsequently as a result of the changes that happen when someone has a child. Take each stage as a different journey and plan for it; the preparations, the time on leave and the return to work. Remember, at each stage people might be different, and have different feelings and expectations, as their identities shift.

The things to remember as a manager are:

- It is absolutely critical to understand your reactions and expectations of the maternity, paternity or adoption transition.

- Don't make assumptions; ask the individual going on leave and your team what they are thinking and feeling.

- The more proactively and positively you communicate the more likely you are to manage this transition effectively.

- Make sure you are clear on your company policies and practices – they are all different.

- Use HR to support you as and when necessary.

- Coaching can be a great way to support individuals going through this transition and to help them to maintain their performance.